Are We There Yet?

Are We There Yet?

Poems by

Ellen Goldsmith

Cover design by Shay Culligan
Cover image entitled *The Wonder of Birds,*
monotype by Cathy Melio
Author photo by Vic Goldsmith

ISBN: 978-1-63980-843-4
Library of Congress Control Number: 2026935160

Kelsay Books
502 South 1040 East, A-119
American Fork, Utah 84003
Kelsaybooks.com

For Vic and Emily
For so many reasons

Acknowledgments

Grateful acknowledgments to the journals, anthologies and newspapers in which some versions of these poems have appeared.

Journals:

Antiphon: “Perfectly Still”
Bellevue Literary Review: “I Am Not Who I Was”
Connecticut River Review: “Out of the Shadows—”
Dash Literary Journal: “Three Tangerines”
Earth’s Daughters: “In the Quiet”
Evening Street Review: “Echocardiogram,” “Edging,” “Mid-March Rain,” “Not Knowing”
The Healing Muse: “A Day Will Come,” “I Am Now an Understudy,” “I’m Writing”
Intima: “In Conversation with Milosz’s *Ars Poetica?*”
Maine Arts Journal: “Trauerarbeit”
Midcoast Poetry Journal: “Deadlines,” “End of Summer,” “On the Way to Lubec,” “The Voice on the Radio”
Mount Hope: “All at Once”
Muddy River Review: “What We Want”
Off the Coast: “Swimming”
Pedestal: “When the Rules Change”
Rhino: “Shavings” as “Hints”
Seven Circle Press: “Back to the View,” “You Never Know,” “When the Snow Doesn’t Last”
Third Wednesday: “Deep Water,” “Out of Control”
Tipton Poetry Journal: “Leading the Discussion for *Enter Ghost* by Isabella Hammad for my Temple Book Group on Sunday January 21, 2024”
Two Hawks Quarterly: “Waiting”

The Westchester Review: "What I Learned from Time in Closets," "Silence," "The Year I Lived with My Grandmother"
The Whirlwind Review: "Each Splash"

Anthologies:

Defiance! Maine Poets Hear America Calling: "The Enemy Within"
Enough: Poems of Resistance and Protest: "Changing the Metaphors," "When I Didn't Protest"
Wait: Poems from the Pandemic: "April 2020"

Newspapers:

Deep Water, Portland Press Herald: "Whatever's Offered," "Navigating New Waters," "Coexistence"
PenBay: Pilot: "Walden"

Appreciation to friends and fellow poets whose insightful reading has improved my poems and enriched this manuscript. Thanks in particular to Judith Carpenter, Kathleen Ellis, Pamela Hall Evans, Vic Goldsmith, Carolyn Locke and Sandy Weisman. For help with the cover image, thanks to John Paul Caponigro.

Contents

II. As We Wait . . .

III. You Never Know

The Wonder of Birds

after a monotype by Cathy Melio

They fly from feeder to tree,
their motion and stillness
capturing us. We wish they'd stay
still so we could name them.

A yellow road winds up the hill,
like an eel snaking through water.
Night birds swoop and glide—
on the other side, birds of light, of day.

Yesterday, shore birds suddenly sprinkled
the sky, moving together in silence,
then turned and were scarcely visible,
like the part of a dream that stays a shadow.

Let these birds—the dark and the light—
fly though our dreams to tangle and untangle
our certainties, our mysteries
so we rise in the morning wondering.

I. Hints

Whatever's Offered

As I listen to Beethoven's late quartets,
I find silence
is not the absence of sound.

Eyes close.

Time vanishes.

I vow
to take whatever's offered—
a crack in the wall, the smaller piece of pie.

In the Quiet

She embraces the gift of calla lilies,
thinks of all she's about to lose.

Later in the day, rain comes
and the memory of a great thirst.

The rose-breasted grosbeak flies away
as she vows to let old grudges go.

In the quiet, she hears the words
her husband isn't saying.

What We Want

What we want is to be like words
that are more than one part of speech,
maybe both noun and verb
like *work* or *spring.*

What we want is to be in the middle
of things—our parents at a movie,
a dream going in different directions,
a cup of coffee.

We want to be like a bird, a fish,
maybe a tiger in how we choose.
And some of us, at some point, want
to stop wanting.

In the Mirror

I lift my arm and see
my mother's wrinkled flesh.
Years ago, naked
in front of another mirror,
I touched my breast
and felt a lump.

Mirror, mirror on the wall . . .

I'm Writing

to tell you the ride
from coast to coast
was jagged

to tell you sometimes
baby steps take you where
you need to go

and I'm finding
illumination
in road signs

Yield, Crossroads
Ahead, Slippery
When Wet—

and I'm writing
to tell you
time rides

in the fast lane
and in the slow lane
and I'm riding in both

Three Tangerines

The trunk in the attic holds the props.
Scarves swirl around and keep saying,
You never know. You never knew.
Tea sets and dolls, out of reach.

The moon is not
out of reach.
When I wake
in the night
its reflection
rests
in the cove.

Three tangerines on a turquoise plate hold
the family secrets.

The Year I Lived with My Grandmother

That year stays like the smell of marigolds on my fingers.
Behind grandmother's warnings against strangers and forgetting

my gloves, I hear the steady hum of blood in blackberries,
the rustle of black widow spiders in brown paper bags.

On my tenth birthday, grandmother covers her eyes with her hands
and calls to my dead grandfather: "Return. It's time."

I fall asleep to the sound of palominos below my window.
In dreams, peacocks wearing gold necklaces call me outside.

Behind rows of fences, lives unfold like horses galloping
or grass growing. Everything is wind, invisible and moving.

Hints

Once I put time in a suitcase with twelve silk scarves.

When I returned to my first house,
no hint of us, only a pink kitchen.

In every mirror, I look so much better than in any photo.

I just noticed.
It's missing from my earring box, a tiny diamond earring,
chipped from my dead grandfather's ring,
passed on to me when my father died.

In my house, half the rooms don't have doors,
and all the doors are half open.

All at Once

From a tree hollowed by lightning,
an arm rises, commanding the view.

A group of rocks becomes a rolling wave.
Crows lift from the lawn all at once.

Last night my dream was holding bird seed.
It all slipped into a crack in the road.

A homemade swing, ropes attached to trees,
the wooden seat uncomfortable, but who cares

when each push adds height and speed.
And then, too soon, feet scrape the earth.

Back Burner

I love when
hard things
slide
to the back burner

when harsh words from last week
lighten
like cake batter
as meringue is folded in

when worry about my eye
rests
for now—
an egg in a nest

Layers

Lately, a speckled bird on my shoulder—
invisible to others—both praises and warns,
trills when I venture beyond my borders,
shrieks when I retreat from kindness.

Last night, snow added a layer
to the outstretched branch of the ash
dividing it in two.
Still, it remains one branch.

Truth

1
Do you tell it?
In a whisper or a shout?
Whose truth? For whose sake?

2
Someone asks *How are you?*
My lips stay sealed for a while
like a hard-to-open jar.
Then I see a multiple-choice test:
    a. OK
    b. Fine
    c. A catalog of what hurts
    d. All of the above

3

When my daughter was in a rough patch,
she went into detail with everyone.
Feeling fine then, I wondered why tell all.
It's taken me years to catch up to her answer:
If I don't say how I feel, I'm being inauthentic.

4

The phone rings.
I'll tell my friend I'm on the deck,
watching the tide recede
and shooing squirrels away from the feeder.

A Deeper Truth

after Robert Browning's *Rabbi Ben Ezra*

Grow old along with me.
The best is yet to be.

With tears in his eyes,
my father intoned these words

at Friday night dinners,
looking lovingly at my mother.

With many surgeries behind me
and another to come,

it is easy for me to disagree.
And yet.

As my parents' bodies diminished
their love grew.

My husband doesn't quote Browning,
but in his eyes I see

what's in my eyes and heart.
Not like muscle, love grows.

The Voice on the Radio

is telling the story of a man wrongfully imprisoned for years
who never loses sight of who he is.

And the words speak to me
a month after a hard surgery
when the self I rely on
has been taken over by pain and exhaustion
and two days after finally having an almost-decent-sleep.

All of me is listening to the details of this terrible injustice
and I ask myself how to resist losing sight of who I am.

Balance

Every day I practice the balancing exercise—
30 seconds on each leg, twice a day.
My left leg is steadier, so each time I ask
if I want to go from hard to easy or easy to hard.

Say the word *balance.*
Note the equal strength in sound
and weight between the two syllables
and how the whole word takes time.

At the ballet, the leaps and turns bring gasps
and applause. I most admire the moments
of balance between movements—
the waiting, the stillness, the holding.

Hopscotch

1
Ghosts inhabit
the places I hardly visit—
the attic and the closet full
of art that hung in our last house.

2
My daughter calls and asks,
Do you know what day it is?
Not the first time I've forgotten
her anniversary.

And I've never told her, her wedding
was the same date I married her father.
Only 7 when the marriage ended,
she hadn't tuned in to that anniversary.

3
Hopscotch requires two skills—
hopping of course
but also
balancing on one leg.

Coexistence

1
One window frames a winter scene.
Bare branches.
Yet in the field, the burnt orange of oaks.
Dislocation and connection.

2
Last summer, standing at the edge of the cove
where I no longer swim,
I felt myself gliding along the shore,
the water a brisk caress,
my body buoyant.

3
It's a mystery I embrace,
how my present reality coexists
with how my body moved decades ago.

It's so much more than the memory
of leaping across the floor in dance class,
of sliding through water in the cove.

When the Snow Doesn’t Last

Like a rare bird’s visit
Gone before I take it in

Before I put words
to the shape of its tail

Gone like rooms
of childhood

Did blinds or curtains
block the morning sun?

I never asked my father
how his father died

Inside, Looking Out

Tree trunks so solid
Branches sway

A blue jay splashes in the bird bath
Abandoned, the water quiets

What disappears?
What remains?

Variations

My friend Monique puts
all kinds of punctuation

in her poems
^^^) (!!! ^^^

I can too!!

&

Birds on the feeder /
and on the railing /
/
They peck and hop /
then fly /

&

Years ago I cracked the shell
and slid out ========================

But escape
isn't easy

So much returns

On the Way to Lubec

1
A lone rock rests
on blueberry barrens

Light touches everything
the way

a Copeland melody
brightens the air

2
I say to my husband
I am wanting

to make more room
for silence

3
We stop at Quoddy Head
stand still

at land's edge until
rushing water quiets

End of Summer

In the cracked bowl
three sizes of tomatoes—
small, medium and large.
Like my hopes,
my disappointments.

An August sky, empty
except for the hawk
alternating between
effortless soaring
and energetic flapping.

It's a warm day, sun as strong
as hummingbirds' desire
for sugar water.
I sit still in the still air.
I sit still in the breeze.

Each Splash

1
I could have sworn the detective in *Crime and Punishment*
appeared on many pages. Not so.
King Lear? Not always there.
A lot about the dukes—Cornwall and Albany.
And I didn't recall Albany's change of heart.
Or was it an unexpected appearance of decency?

2
An open-door policy—
immigration, trade, the bedroom.
Is that what the man in the moon wants?

3
When we're finished with school,
we're free to skip parts of long novels—
the war in *War and Peace* for example—
but we're outraged
if pages are missing.

4
If I could skip a stone,
my hand on shore
would feel each splash
as a revelation.

Roses

For a surprise, my husband brings me roses—
peach with hints of yellow, orange and pink.
I choose a Lenox China vase for its cream color
and the way its shape allows the roses to reach out.

Each morning, I snip the ends and change the water.
I want them to last.
Each morning, no matter how careful I am,
a thorn pierces a finger.

This morning, the Day of Atonement,
I do this task before leaving for Temple.
I'm extra careful as I take the stem.
Still, flesh meets thorn.

A Day Will Come

when the heirloom watch is beyond
repair

when the rare illness can't be
cured

when the confidence in a better tomorrow
dies.

But today, snow on the field brightens
the browns and grays and dark greens

and the daffodils my husband brought home yesterday say *love*

and I feel the patience of bulbs
that will push through the damp and dark

to greet spring and I hold, not tight
but gently, these words—

a day will come.

II. As We Wait . . .

Waiting

isn’t a room. It’s the whole house.

I Am Now an Understudy

for the part I was to play this spring

A flurry of cancellations—
classes book groups Passover Seder
No entrance to places I would have inhabited
Instead, I move from room to room
straightening
as I can't
the mess of the virus

And what's under study—how
to stay steady, how
to replace the term for what we're doing—
physical not social distancing—how
to find pleasure—more time for baking and walking—
without eclipsing the dark source
of this new-found time. How
to go deeper
into the mystery of time—
taking time saving time losing time.
And what of the eleventh hour?

I remember the long car rides, how
my parents laughed
when before even entering
the Holland Tunnel, I would ask,
Are we there yet?

The Mystery of During

It might be interminable
or short

You don’t know until afterwards
if it was a cave or a cove

Some *durings* are as comfortable
as well-worn but not worn-out shoes

Others test the mettle with how
much of the self slips into hiding

Contingent

The word is always there—
sometimes backstage
other times hiding
in the winter coat closet.
And then it rises—
a blinding sun
when a new unexplained pain
makes its debut
and you can't do the ordinary.
You can't meet a friend for coffee,
take a walk, sweep the floor.
The pain like a powerful
vacuum sweeps everything up.

April 2020

Snow furiously descends
on this 25th day of sheltering in place,
the landscape transformed
as if I've traveled to another continent
or slid backwards into winter.
I hardly recall when we could assemble
for dinner in a restaurant.
It's 6 a.m. and time stretches.
For now, I sit at the window
in silence as tree branches and field
receive their white covering.
It is so steady, this falling
of large flakes. I can imagine
them falling forever.

Pneumonia

My body has become
the music box—
my best gift
at my 9th birthday party—
but I no longer
recognize the tune
and the dancer
has lost her grace.

Hospital Sleep

At midnight
I turn off the light
and wait to sink into sleep.

I lie still
and see myself
on the table in the operating room.

The table becomes the branch
of our white pine
at shore's edge.

It's outstretched
ready
for the osprey

and for me
to be lifted
into sleep

As He Waits for Test Results

I tell my friend Irene my husband is listening
to Rachmaninoff, Brahms, Beethoven, Mendelssohn—
a concerto, then a symphony, next a fantasy.
Doesn't he always listen to music? she asks.

I don't have the words for this listening,
how the notes and silences, harmonies
and dissonances hold and release
beauty and darkness beyond words.

The Closet

Yesterday, my husband complained
about the disorder of so many shoes

cluttering the hallway, including four pairs
of sandals I won't wear for months.

So I bagged them, took them downstairs,
set them outside the closet.

Not that I don't have time
to line them up inside but because

I'm not ready to open the door.

Echocardiogram

1
I watched my heart
during my first
echo, loved how
it never
stops.

2
This time, I know something's wrong
when the tech needs to consult
the doctor. *Don't leave,* she instructs.
I don't.
Heart beating fast,

I wait.

3
A stiff heart—
aortic stenosis
in medical jargon.
Younger, my body
was so flexible,
a backbend easy as pie.
And now it's my mind
turning over and over
in a flood of cartwheels.

Navigating New Waters

1

The roofers are banging
and machines whir.
Most windows are covered and all doors
blocked.

Where I can see out—
ladders, blue drop cloths, ropes, old shingles
strewn
across the lawn.

No leaks yet
but shingles, worn and misshapen.

2

In my other house,
severe stenosis of my aortic valve.

3
Windy today.
I hold tight to the paper as I write
so it won't blow away.

4
A small boy wheels his bicycle
to the bluff at the edge of the water.

Wait, I call.

What I'm Learning from the Light

I wake to light
after the dark and wind
of yesterday

and it's as if
my body is turning
from gray to gold.

On the wooden floor,
I see my recovery—
a mix of shine and shadow.

I Am Not Who I Was

My illness, rare as a blue moon,
a place I look back on, unsettled
like frontier territory. I lived
there but wasn't acquainted,
had no map.

Today, the air is perfectly clear,
my familiar view heightened
into a super-realist painting.

Trees startle. Leaves
flutter like grace notes.

Interruptions

A cloud interrupts clear sky.
A wave interrupts calm water.
Illness interrupts life.

For years, my friend Susan has been praising
the ruptures of disease and surgery
as opportunities.

I did not concur.
What use these *breaches,*
suspensions, obstructions, intrusions?

And now
less threatening words come—
hiatus, intermission, parenthesis.

I think of how in a painting
the almost empty corner
brings the central swirl to life.

An Answer to a Question

You ask what's my favorite word

I'm silent for a while even though I know

Then I say *spacious*

And become my field in winter, snow-covered

With a pattern of shadows

Coming to Terms

is a gate
and then another gate.

Think of how as the decades roll by
what was just an incline has become a hill
and how you always reach for the banister.

But it's not just that.
You've poured boiling water
into the wrong bowl
and your husband has forgotten
about the baking chicken.
You both forgive.

Yesterday you learned
a friend has an aggressive brain cancer.
She speaks of her faith
which may open a gate for her.

Is it a matter of choice
to see the gate opening or closing?

In Conversation with Milosz's *Ars Poetica?*

Poetry, you say, is a reminder of how hard it is to remain
only one person. When I was a different person, the sick me,
was that a narrowing of self or someone else entirely?

The door to my hospital room was always open
and I beckoned to whoever walked by,
doctor and patient alike.

*

A swirl of selves. The-getting-sick-me surprised
at how hard it was to unload the dishwasher.
The me in the doctor's office or in the CT scanner,
failing every test. The empty-riverbed-me,
accepting whatever came.
And then the coming-into-spring-me,
thrilled by the smallest gain—
being able to go up and down three steps.

*

As I look at the world outside my window,
the words recovery and healing come forward
like your *invisible guests.*

The wind moves
everything, the thin branches of the birch,
the needle-laden boughs of the white pine.

Like you, I aspire to *a more spacious form.*
Perhaps a leafless tree revealing a starry sky.
Perhaps an evergreen, steady with holding on.

III. You Never Know

Swimming

Lately, I'm seeing poems as places to put things. Moments that haven't dissolved but haven't yet found their own poem. So they ask to stop floating around like dust in the air or debris on the water. Like when I swam and swam and swam in Lake Michigan, kept going because every other lake I'd been in I could swim to the other side. And after a while I was so tired, not sure I could swim back to shore. But I did. And it wouldn't be right to reduce the experience to a one-sentence-main-idea. In my sixth-grade-Friday-afternoon club, we played *Five Objects.* One of us hid these small things in plain sight so a penny disappeared into the design of a plate. I liked it best when I couldn't separate the object from its new home.

You Never Know

There are a number of recordings in my head. When I leave the house, my mother's voice suggests I bring another sweater, *just in case,* quickly followed by *you never know.* This is true more often than not, not just about the temperature. For example, what attracted me to my first boyfriend, his charm, had a negative underside. At this moment, I can't put my finger on the exact name of the underside of charm, so I'm imagining the word hiding somewhere in my brain, maybe stuck against French vocabulary. And I'm thinking about the brain and memory storage and even though it's unscientific, I'm picturing drains in the brain which can clog up. Maybe memory has a will of its own and sometimes tires of performing, like the Rockettes must have sometimes wanted to stop kicking up their legs in perfect unison.

Deep Water

I asked my daughter a question and before she uttered a word, I was formulating her answer. I cringed at the limits of my listening. And now the radio's talking about deep listening, and I'm feeling that sudden drop from shallow to deep, feeling my body shifting from vertical to horizontal, remembering the few times in the water when I've stopped being me and become a fish. To really listen I need to leave myself behind, on a shelf or in a drawer. Speaking of drawers, the only good thing about Sunday visits to my grandmother's house on Stone Avenue—opening the special drawer in mysterious and always absent Aunt Leah's room to find surprises. A clothespin doll. Aquamarine hard candy. A rusty key.

Back to the View

I sit with my back to the water. In front of me the forest. Not really a full-fledged forest but holding a lot of shade although sunlight creeps in where the branches aren't growing. My mind wanders and an old memory materializes. It must happen to you too, something that doesn't seem significant enough to come back but it does. For example, in sixth grade, walking up the steps to the Garden Court Apartments, I thought if my life were a movie, this would be the boring part. Or the day at Jones Beach when my father fell asleep with his leg sticking out from the umbrella and the sun burned it.

Out of Control

On the way out of the golf club cocktail party, I catch myself in a mirror. My hair is so out of control. Like on that blind date in college when I could hardly return from the bathroom to the Tom, Dick or Harry I was with, my hair such a horrible frizz. And I ask my husband when we're out and my hair is a mess to tell me. He says he likes the windswept look. Clearly, I can't count on him. Hair out of control makes me think about body parts making their own decisions. Wrinkles which come on their own time and freckles which I don't have. But what I did have was a breast that allowed a tumor to grow.

After the Organ Recital

In my dream, I'm the one chosen to bring the organ back to the music school where it belongs. *Only give it to Mr. Owen,* I'm told.

The music school isn't far. A ramshackle house with a blue door that opens with a tap. I find myself in the Teacher's Lounge, full of sounds—the whir of the copy machine, different registers of laughter, music with an insistent bass. I ask the nearest person where I can find Mr. Owen. *Not here. He slips around.*

Suddenly, I'm walking down an overgrown path in a dense forest at daybreak or dusk and I don't have the organ.

Eachother

The point is we use different words for the same thing or use the same words for different things and I think back to one of the *you were so cute* stories my parents told, the one where I was listening to them talk and they must have said something like, *Don't worry. We'll look out for each other.* And I asked, *What's eachother?* They told this story until the day they died. My father, at home at midnight just after returning from forty-three horrible days in the hospital. And my mother, six years later, in the hospital when I left her bedside for a lunch break, a month before 9/11. I was glad she didn't have to worry about me stranded in Brooklyn. When the subway was running again how crazy it was when I ended up at Times Square rather than Grand Central. Not such a big deal to get from one to the other. Nothing compared to a plane flying into a building.

You Shouldn't Know You Have a Foot

is one of my grandmother's sayings, handed down to me. It made sense in a general way. And now it's quite specific because almost all the time, for a number of reasons including hammer toes, I feel one foot or the other. I hated Sunday visits to my grandmother's house. She dragged around in a drab house dress, didn't hug or kiss me, hardly said a word to me. But I didn't complain because I knew the visits did something for my mother. Never asked what. Now it's on a growing list of questions I call *What I Should Have Asked Before They Died.*

Four-Leaf Clover

My daughter's friend said she needs to work on her eye-hand coordination to draw better. And I said it's about seeing. Really seeing. Not just looking and saying *tree* to oneself but seeing the actual shapes, each separate part and the dynamics of attachment. And then I remembered searching for four-leaf clovers, those summer afternoons when my sister and I planted ourselves on patch after patch of overgrown grass. Our fingers delicately separated and then our eyes investigated. The thrill when the rare one appeared. An *anything-is-possible* moment. I loved when I first met *all-of-the-above* on a multiple-choice test. After that, I was disappointed with tests with only one right answer.

Retrieval

I'm coming and going from *The Washington Post* Sunday crossword puzzle which I'm trying for the first time. And I should be filling in more because the hint is obvious—*men and women of note whose last name is a U.S. president.* Yet so many boxes are still empty, and I'm realizing my retrieval is much slower than it used to be. That jazz singer with the last name of a president is at least a New York City Avenue block away, perhaps the distance from Lexington to Park. While I'm waiting, I recall the day I came home from school in tears. When my mother asked what was wrong, I said, "the teacher yelled." She asked what I did. "Nothing. One of the boys ripped up someone's homework." What was *his* name? Suddenly from deep storage, Diana Washington sings *Unforgettable.*

Out of the Shadows—

Like what happens when I stand before a painting, let's say a seascape with a rosy sky and gold-streaked clouds entitled "Broad Cove" and I can't tell if it's sunrise or sunset. I love that. When the back story and the future don't matter the way one line from an Auden poem—*About suffering they were never wrong*—has an independent existence. And don't you think some melodies from symphonies have existed forever and Dvorak and Copland just found them?

Perfectly Still

Remember the genie who grants three wishes and how people waste their wishes. I'm thinking of a genie who'd answer three questions. One would be why when you sit in a chair right after someone gets up it's warm, but when you sit back down in your own chair, it doesn't feel warm. I'd ask that first even though the answer might be some principle of physics or chemistry I could look up. I'd ask it first rather than the meaning of life, which I'd like to know especially in light of the horrors of history and the fact of death. But I'm not sure I like the idea of only one meaning of life. At least that's what I think now, 5 a.m., looking out at the field rimmed by trees leading down to a foggy cove where sky and water are the same pearl gray. Indistinguishable. And it might be perfectly quiet. And it is perfectly still.

What I Learned from Time in Closets

The rule of hide and seek: wait until you're found. And I followed rules so there I was, in a dark hall closet, waiting, waiting for such a long time until finally I opened the door and heard happy voices and laughter in the playroom.

Don't wait too long.

Alone in the cold house, I snuggled in the hall closet with my mother's mouton and my father's wool coat, warm and cozy until I reached for the knob to open the door. It had none.

Check your exit plan.

Silence

In poetry class, we were talking about *The Portrait* by Stanley Kunitz, how it holds the story of his mother slapping him for retrieving a picture of the father he never knew, the father who committed suicide before he was born. And suddenly my father's story hit me, his father found dead on the subway tracks. *Jumped or was pushed,* the newspaper reported, the year 1929. This unknown grandfather, some kind of businessman. My father, 12 years old.

I hear silence in my father's Washington Heights apartment, too loud for laughter. All those years, the not-telling was a silence in my row house in Queens. A secret that didn't entice me, so busy with the claims of my life.

When I was no longer living at home, a photo of an elegant and melancholy man with my father's eyes and fuller lips suddenly claimed space on my father's dresser. An image returned from the dead. Was it hiding all those years under the socks?

In some quartets, silence is a bridge to beauty. What if towards the end of the second movement, the musicians put down their bows and the silence went on and on—

Deadlines

I was talking to my friend Judith about how I'm loving *David Copperfield,* a book group book, very long and I need to finish in a week. So I'm using in-between-times, like while the quiche is baking or when I'm waiting for a friend to arrive at FlipSide. Thinking about today and where there's open time to sit with David and his disappointment with Dora, the word *deadline* comes to mind. I disagree with such a downbeat word for something that gives shape and purpose. I can't imagine what makes a line dead. After all, one line follows another and makes a paragraph. And when the paragraph ends, there's someplace else to go.

In the Wine Seller in Rockland, Maine

I was browsing when a woman eagerly approached me and said, “I love your earrings! I have a pair by the same designer.” “I doubt it,” I said. “I got them in Carefree, Arizona.” And she said, “So did I.” And we went on to reminisce about the quirky Mexican restaurant in the shopping center and how it’s shopping center after shopping center from Phoenix to Carefree. I love coincidences. More even than rainbows. The way they bring the unlikely into a large arena holding astrophysicists and cowboys, where you can press a button to turn night into day.

Show and Tell

was my favorite part of Friday in elementary school,
my week shaped by searching for an object

interesting to look at, with a story attached.
Best of all was a pin that perched on my mother's dresser,

a bird in flight, wings studded with rhinestone chips.
When I asked why she never wore it, she said

using it would undo the magic of how it flew into her life.
A salesgirl in Lord and Taylor's Costume Jewelry Department,

she waited on an elegant woman who was buying many gifts.
Pin after pin, a necklace, bracelet after bracelet went into

small silver boxes. Choosing complete, she asked my mother
if she worked there full-time. *No, just part-time to help pay*

for my upcoming wedding. The woman reexamined the case,
then pointed to a pin of a blue bird.

My mother handed it to her and she gave it back
to my mother saying, "This bluebird of happiness

is my wedding gift to you." Poetry teachers say show,
don't tell. But sometimes isn't the telling what is telling?

IV. You Know

Paving the Driveway

I wake to a reverberating thump

Outside, the paving machine spreads asphalt
This winter the snowplow won't throw dirt
on the garden or lawn

For some things there's no fixing—

how my legs no longer run
how a terrorist attack changes everything
how sometimes there's nothing
to cover up the dirt

To Change the Metaphors

That's why we're toppling Confederate Monuments.
Replacing the Mississippi flag.
Rethinking the mission of police departments.
Unearthing the underbelly of our prejudices.

At my daughter's college graduation,
the speaker addressed inequality and the racial divide.
We can look at it, he said, as a cigarette burn
on your linen tablecloth and cover it up
with an embroidered napkin. Or we can see it
for what it is—fault lines under the earth's surface.

Are the murders of Eric Garner and George Floyd
what the fault lines were waiting for?
Are we who are not black or brown listening
more deeply to the truths of slavery, hearing
the moans of loss along with the words
I can't breathe.

When I came to the coast, I was entranced
by the tides, their regularity, their promise of return.
Now, I reject the back and forth of the tides of history,
want to embrace a new metaphor. A carrier pigeon
not stopping until the message is delivered.

Mid-March Rain

You ask about the weather
and I answer even though
I don't want to talk
about the weather.

I want to talk about Ukraine.
Not really.
But it's a spill on the tablecloth,
blotting out the everyday.

Instead of bird song,
I hear the rumble of tanks,
cries of children.
I feel the pain of leaving
everything behind.

Back in time
at my grandmother's kitchen table in Brooklyn,
I bite into her challah, sip my coffee-milk,
listen to the Yiddish I don't understand.
Again and again, *The Ukraine, The Ukraine.*
What's the Ukraine? I ask my mother.

A place that didn't want your grandmother

Leading the Discussion for *Enter Ghost* by Isabella Hammad for the Temple Book Group on Sunday, January 21, 2024

Right afterwards, I have a workshop
on creating tension in poems.
I'm nervous about the discussion. Tense.
A book from the Palestinian perspective at Books and Bagels.
As I drive to the temple on a day of strong snow flurries
but cleared roads I interrogate myself.
Where in my body is the tension?

Enter Ghost, the last words of the novel,
invite in King Hamlet's ghost
who will command Hamlet
to seek justice in his rotten kingdom.
In this play within a play within a novel,
actors perform *Hamlet* in classical Arabic
on the West Bank. It's set in 2017
when two Israeli police officers were killed
at the Temple Mount. Now, months after
the horrific events of October 7th,
will it be hard for some to open the doors of empathy?

Leaving the house, I had a back and forth on whether
to add grippers to my boots.
To protect or not to protect . . .

Questions hide under my coat.
What was it like for my grandfather growing up in Palestine?
What are my ghosts concocting?

The Enemy Within

can’t carry a tune
buries cacophony
in other organs

where it stays in place
developing expertise
in uncovering weakness

until it strikes
then plans
what’s next

On Tyranny: Twenty Lessons from the Twentieth Century

is the book I finished just before turning in tonight. My dream begins with rushing out of the house to get to the book discussion group. I jump on a red scooter and zip along the road, arrive at the house, no place to park so I leave the scooter down the road. Disarray downstairs. Loud voices upstairs. I climb up, bunches of people, none of whom I know. I take off my coat and see that I'm wearing my bathrobe over my clothes. "Oh well," I think and throw it down over my coat. Then I realize I don't have the book, tell the discussion leader who says I need to go back home to get it. "I'll take my robe," I think. I don't remember where my scooter is, finally find it but now it's blue. As I ride back, I think of my grandparents in the Ukraine, relatives in Jerusalem. And all of us in a darkening world.

To Adrienne Rich

after Adrienne Rich's *An Atlas of the Difficult World*

Your map of our country travels
into hidden corners, places where most only see
a family portrait on the wall, everyone smiling,
not the sad faces after the photographer has snapped.

You paid attention to spiders
admired how they use everything
to spin a house within a house.

Do we start with maps and stretch to an atlas?
When we see over fences and beyond
do we enter atlas territory?

And what about the difference between the map
and actual place that surprises with potholes
and specimen trees, sharp curves
and sudden vistas?

Once, on a plane from New York to San Francisco
I saw you. You wrote furiously the whole flight.
At the carousel, you asked my husband
to grab your suitcase before it went round again.

Not Knowing

after Merwin's "For the Anniversary of My Death"

In Merwin's poem, the rain ends and
he is bowing, not knowing to what.

On the date her mother died my sister-in-law drinks
martinis and makes her mother's mushroom turnovers.

I celebrate the dates my parents were born,
how my mother would burst into song
like Mary Martin in *South Pacific,*
how my father's laughter
delayed the punch line of any joke he told.

Merwin calls life "a strange garment."
I see Joseph's coat of many colors.
The coat—a gift from his father Jacob.
Life—a gift we wrap and unwrap.

June 2020, sheltered in place by the pandemic,
I take stock of what's around me—
water rippling to shore, an ant carrying
a crumb, a tree felled by the last storm.

When I Didn't Protest

Just out of college, I was an English teacher at a Brooklyn high school, late afternoon classes full of students counting the days until they could drop out. Nothing in the conventional textbook sparked a response. So I looked around and found *That Word Black* by Langston Hughes which ends with the question, "What's wrong with black?"

In those days, we submitted lesson plans in advance. For the first time, the chair of the department called me into her office. She told me I couldn't present that rabble-rousing essay. And I didn't.

Today, so much older, I reexamine the essay, marvel at its insight into the power of words, into how the unexamined can oppress. It makes a case for giving the word *black* the beauty of earth, which is black.

It suggests making white bad.

There is no going back to the 22-year-old who didn't argue, didn't take the risk of disobedience.

I am writing this to sign on to speaking out, taking the risk and so whoever reads this poem looks back and looks forward.

was the homework for my evening class at a community college where I was new and the students came to class tired from a hard day's work. Tired, but they did the reading. And I was tired too because my house was being painted and I felt weighed down by too many coffee table photography books and more dishes than I could ever use. So after the inspirational "Only that day dawns to which we are awake," I read quotes like "A man is rich in proportion to the number of things which he can afford to let alone" and ". . . my greatest skill has been to want but little." And I had more.

But you know how you can feel people leaving the room even though they're there, how their bodies empty out and everything that makes them vital recedes beyond the back wall. So I stopped with my quotes and asked what was going on.

After some silence one man said something like, "Lady, you may feel weighed down by stuff, but we don't have a lot. We want more. Doubles, triples even."

And then it was my time to be silent and the silence took me into a new knowing.

When the Rules Change

Once, I heard the clang of prison gates.

There to give a workshop, I was required
to walk through the metal detector.
The guard asked me to remove my earrings.
Not necessary, I said. *I don't at the airport.*
He gave me a withering look.
As I walked through, my earrings screamed.

When the rules change,
it's like a strong wind blows
and all the trees are swaying.
Then the trees stop swaying
but the wind still blows.

Gender Matters

A friend and I were parading
our baby carriages, my little one in pink,
hers in blue. A neighbor peeked in.

She greeted my daughter, "Hello,
you delicate little girl," and to my friend's son,
"Hello, you big strong boy."

•

After I lost my breasts, I enjoyed
the lightness of a flat chest.
Sometimes an arrow struck,
like the Christmas windows at Saks Fifth Avenue—
one elegant woman after another in satin and velvet gowns.

All I saw was cleavage.

•

Kathleen tells me her college recommends
when in doubt
to use the pronoun *they* for everyone.
Some people object.
Remember when Ms.
was an affront to some?

How Much Can I Hold?

November 2023, the start of the Israel/Hamas War

Mary Alice advises me
when going up and down stairs
carrying the laundry or books
to put them in a shoulder bag
so my hands are free.

On the radio, an historian
is talking about genocide,
giving his opinion on
who is committing it now.
How do I carry *this?*

Trauerarbeit

after the tapestry of a face by Alan Magee
Trauerarbeit: in German, the work of mourning

1
The face holds the pain.
Eyes, lakes of tears.
Nose, a broken bridge.
The mouth, speechless.
All these blacks and grays, what can they say?

But they must.

2
The work of mourning is to tell the story.
Over and over   At the dinner table   In school
            In casual conversation
The sign at the beginning of the road reads:
This is the route to accept the unacceptable.

3
Last night I watched the movie *Munich,*
saw bombs and guns kill
the Black September terrorists
who killed the Jewish athletes.

To be or not to be.
To kill or not to kill.

4
I wake to the news of another power outage in Gaza
and more deaths.
Heavy fog softens the town.

Breaking the Mirror

after Leonard Baskin's Holocaust woodcuts

It's a Roman myth—seven years bad luck
unless you undo the curse with salt,
circling, or burying the pieces.

Aren't we in the fix we're in
because we've buried so many pieces?
At Lake Mead, a fourth set of human remains
rose as the water level kept dropping.

You've heard the expression,
It's always darkest before the dawn.
But have you seen Baskin's Holocaust series?
Larger than life woodcuts of death—a hulking giant
swollen by evil, fed by indifference.

Baskin holds a cracked mirror for all to see.
Like carefully constructed ambiguous images—
Edgar Rubin's vase for example—once we see
the profiles, it's hard to return to the vase.

Edging

My husband takes a break from edging the garden,
leans on the shovel.
I turn

from the front window to take the measure of our field.
To be in two places at once.
See my husband and also the Queen Anne's lace.

I hear my mother's voice,
think of leaves.
They're there. They leave. They return.

Edging imposes order.
I used to want that
until I visited Mount St. Helen's

ten years after it erupted
and weeds were
the only growing things.

About the Author

Ellen Goldsmith reads, writes, and teaches poetry with equal enthusiasm. Her first full-length manuscript—*Are We There Yet?*—follows four chapbooks. The first, *No Pine Tree in This Forest Is Perfect,* won the 1997 Slapering Hol Chapbook Competition. Dennis Nurkse, the judge, described it as "an incandescent collection." *Left Foot, Right Foot,* the most recent, is an illness and recovery narrative in 28 poems. Carl Little observes, "These unstinting, deftly crafted poems 'contain the mess' that is life."

Goldsmith holds an Ed.D. from Teachers College, Columbia University and is Professor Emerita of the City University of New York. She was on the faculty at two branches of CUNY, John Jay College of Criminal Justice and New York City College of Technology. There, she founded and directed the grant-funded Center for Intergenerational Reading. Its mission was to provide professional development for early childhood teachers preparing them to add family literacy workshops to their schools.

A resident of Cushing Maine, Goldsmith enjoys the rich cultural life of mid-coast Maine where the particular light of day and the bright stars at night console and inspire her.

www.ingramcontent.com/pod-product-compliance
Lightning Source LLC
LaVergne TN
LVHW091012080826
845145LV00003B/1235
9781639808434